MW01618431

For Silas - your curiosity, mischief and kindheartedness inspire me. D.A.

For my cubs - may you always be wild. C.A.

HICCUP MAKES A LEAP

Delfina Aguilar

Clare Aitken

Sabrina Arnault

A *Fanny & Alexander* book

One morning, much like any other morning, Hiccup woke up, like he always did.

But something was different. He needed to find a new career.

There had to be a better profession.

Wherever he went, he felt unwelcome.
People seemed exasperated…

HIC!
OH NO!
GRRR...

Even his friends.
(Maybe especially his friends.)

People even used his name to describe
a plan going awry.

SO?
THERE WAS A BIT OF A HICCUP

The others were happy.

To snotty Sneeze,
people kindly said ‘bless you’.

Dizzy Giggle always got
a warm reception.

Even boisterous Burp got a smile
(from some people).

But Hiccup?
People just tried to scare him away.

Hiccup knew he could be great. He just didn't know at what.

But he was going to find out.

'I'm creative,' Hiccup thought. 'I could do that.'

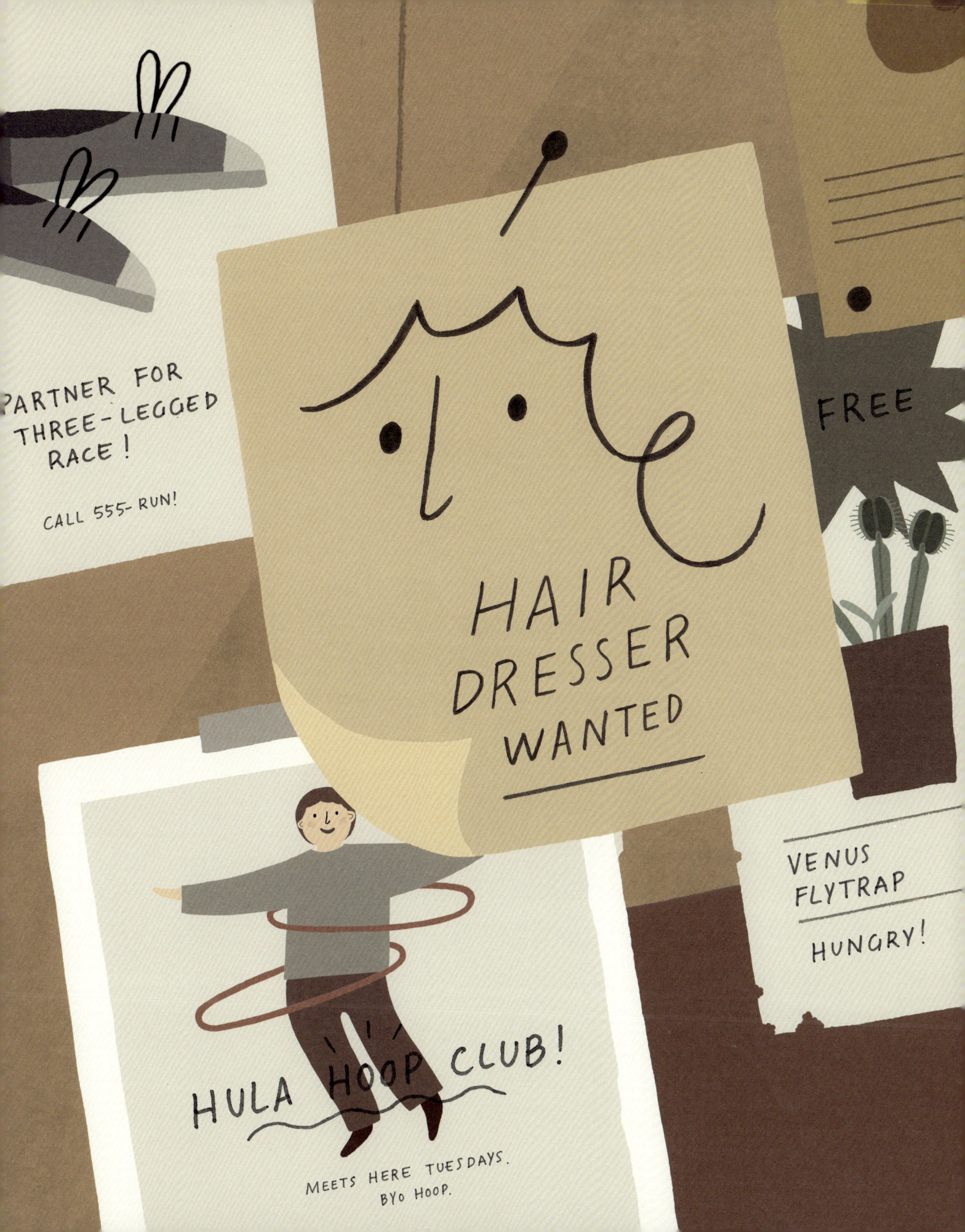

PARTNER FOR
THREE-LEGGED
RACE!

CALL 555-RUN!

HAIR
DRESSER
WANTED

FREE

VENUS
FLYTRAP

HUNGRY!

Hiccup did his best, but his uncontrollable jerks resulted in some truly atrocious haircuts.

HAIRDRESSER

‘Hmm…no scissors,’ Hiccup reasoned.
‘And I am quite artistic…’

PORTRAIT
ARTIST
WANTED

Hiccup tried, but his helpless twitching spurted paint right out of the tubes.

'Less mess,' Hiccup nodded to himself.
'And I am helpful…'

BAO 13:21
HIC!

He concentrated as hard as he could – but another unruly outburst sent food flying everywhere.

'That sounds relaxing,' Hiccup considered. 'And I'm very caring.'

S15
CX8
HT8
LI1
SP3
TH6
A1
A8
E1
D
ST36

Try as he might to stay still, Hiccup erupted – and accidentally turned the patient into a hedgehog.

NATURAL
HISTORY
MUSEUM
CLEANER
NEEDED

‘Dinosaurs can’t get angry,’
Hiccup sniffed.

‘And I’m very clean and tidy…’

At the worst possible moment, another unstoppable HIC! - and disaster - struck.

Well, that proved it: Hiccup was totally, thoroughly, indisputably useless.

'What is the point of me, anyway?', he wondered aloud.

‘Rhetorical or literal question?’
a voice replied.

‘Pardon?’ Hiccup sniffled.

A lady plunked down next to him.

'Literal. Well,' she replied thoughtfully. 'Let's see. The point of you. I suppose the answer is…life.'

'Life?'

HIC!

'Yes – life!' she replied.

'Once, life only existed in the seas, and sea creatures breathed through gills. Until the very first hiccups, approximately 370 million years ago. That was the beginning of breathing on land as well as water – the beginning of life on earth. So – yes – I'd say that's the point of you.'

Hiccup gawped. From totally, thoroughly, indisputably useless to the beginning of life on earth?

It was a lot to take in.

‘So – without hiccups, there wouldn’t be any humans? And…if there weren’t any humans, there wouldn’t be…’ – his mind boggled – ‘…any haircuts, or restaurants, or art? Or even…hide-and-seek?’

‘Correct,’ the learned lady nodded. ‘Your very existence is a reminder of the impossible leap life once made.’

'Th-th-thank you…' Hiccup stammered, feeling very lightheaded as he stumbled away.

He was not only useful.
He was *essential*.

Maybe he'd been thinking about this all wrong.

Maybe happiness wasn't about what he *did* – but who he *was*?

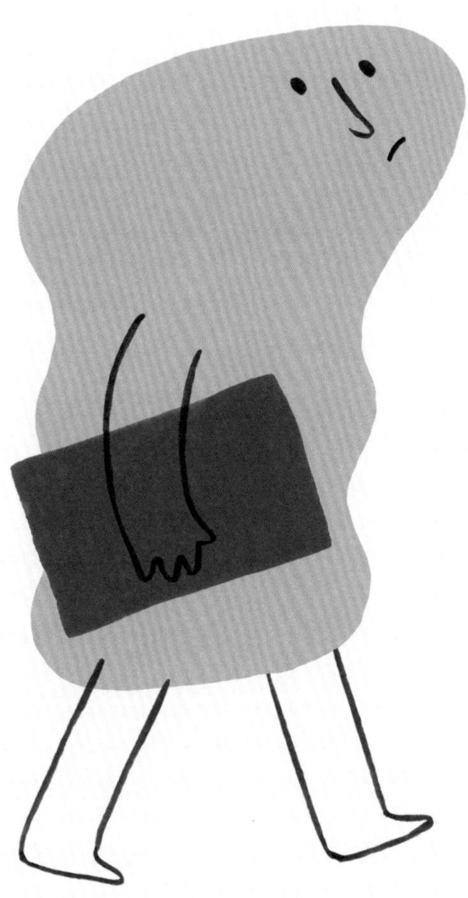

ronnie scott's jazz club
MARCH
ronnie

And who he was, was Hiccup.

And that – as his irrepressible eruptions became part of a jazz melody that jerked and leapt and soared…

HIC!

…turned out to be quite wonderful.

Goodnight.

(HIC!)

Created by: Delfina Aguilar
Writer: Clare Aitken
Illustrator / Designer: Sabrina Arnault
Illustration development: Hiromi Suzuki

First printed edition 2020
ISBN 978-1-9161679-1-9

fannyandalexander.co.uk